Just the Opposite
Big /Small

Exactamente lo opuesto
Grande /Pequeño

Sharon Gordon

 Marshall Cavendish
Benchmark
New York

My bed is big.

❖

Mi cama es grande.

Your bed is small.

Tu cama es pequeña.

My dog is big.

Mi perro es grande.

Your dog is small.

❖

Tu perro es pequeño.

My bus is big.

❖

Mi autobús es grande.

Your bus is small.

❖

Tu autobús es pequeño.

7

My bike is big.

❖

Mi bicicleta es grande.

Your bike is small.

Tu bicicleta es pequeña.

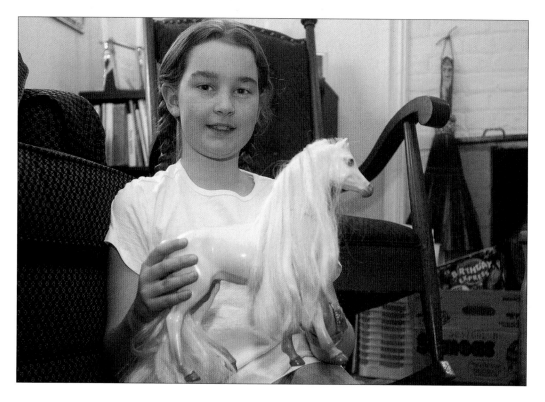

My horse is big.

❖

Mi caballo es grande.

Your horse is small.

❖

Tu caballo es pequeño.

My present is big.

❖

Mi regalo es grande.

Your present is small.

❖

Tu regalo es pequeño.

My ice cream is big.

Mi helado es grande.

Your ice cream is small.

❖

Tu helado es pequeño.

My bubble is big.

❖

Mi globo es grande.

Your bubble is small.

❖

Tu globo es pequeño.

Pop!

❖

¡Pum!

19

Words We Know
Palabras que sabemos

bed
cama

bike
bicicleta

bubble
globo

bus
autobús

20

dog
perro

horse
caballo

ice cream
helado

present
regalo

Index

Page numbers in **boldface** are illustrations.

Índice

Las páginas indicadas con números en **negrita** tienen ilustraciones.

About the Author
Datos biográficos de la autora

Sharon Gordon has written many books for young children. She has always worked as an editor. Sharon and her husband Bruce have three children, Douglas, Katie, and Laura, and one spoiled pooch, Samantha. They live in Midland Park, New Jersey.

❖

Sharon Gordon ha escrito muchos libros para niños. Siempre ha trabajado como editora. Sharon y su esposo Bruce tienen tres niños, Douglas, Katie y Laura, y una perra consentida, Samantha. Viven en Midland Park, Nueva Jersey.

With thanks to Nanci Vargus, Ed.D.
and Beth Walker Gambro, reading consultants

Marshall Cavendish Benchmark
99 White Plains Road
Tarrytown, New York 10591-9001
www.marshallcavendish.us

Library of Congress Cataloging-in-Publication Data

Gordon, Sharon.
[Big small. Spanish & English]
Big small = Grande pequeño / Sharon Gordon. — Bilingual ed.
p. cm. — (Bookworms. Just the opposite = Exactamente lo opuesto)
Includes bibliographical references and index.
ISBN-13: 978-0-7614-2445-1 (bilingual edition : alk. paper)
ISBN-10: 0-7614-2445-8 (bilingual edition : alk. paper)
ISBN-13: 978-0-7614-2364-5 (Spanish edition : alk. paper)
ISBN-10: 0-7614-1568-8 (English edition : alk. paper)
1. Size perception—Juvenile literature. 2. Size judgment—Juvenile literature. I. Title. II. Title: Grande pequeño.
III. Series: Gordon, Sharon. Bookworms. Just the opposite (Spanish & English)

BF299.S5G6718 2006b
153.7'52—dc22
2006017269

Spanish Translation and Text Composition by Victory Productions, Inc.
www.victoryprd.com

Photo Research by Anne Burns Images

Cover Photos by Jay Mallin

The photographs in this book are used with permission and through the courtesy of:
Jay Mallin: pp. 1, 2, 3, 4, 5, 8, 9, 10, 11, 12, 13, 14, 15, 16, 17, 18, 19, 20 (top) (bottom left), 21.
Corbis: p. 6 Tom Stewart; pp. 7, 20 (bottom right) Tom & Dee Ann McCarthy.

Series design by Becky Terhune

Printed in Malaysia
1 3 5 6 4 2